TONY IANTOSCA
TO THE ATTIC

SPUYTEN DUYVIL
New York City

© 2020 Tony Iantosca
ISBN 978-1-952419-17-1

Library of Congress Cataloging-in-Publication Data

Names: Iantosca, Tony, author.
Title: To the attic / Tony Iantosca.
Description: New York City : Spuyten Duyvil, [2020] |
Identifiers: LCCN 2020024330 | ISBN 9781952419171 (paperback)
Subjects: LCGFT: Poetry.
Classification: LCC PS3609.A665 T6 2020 | DDC 811/.6--dc23
LC record available at https://lccn.loc.gov/2020024330

Outrage orphan

Feelings jumble
the scripts
for us to inhabit, say
orphaned outrage
spread wide enough
for a view
so some of us look
from high windows
and others
ignore that. Out past
the gate a body
unknown approaches
holding a phrase
to be recast like train
signals subtracting a train,
the track departs
from branches
to frame stones
consumed words
and lightning
at intermission.
That digestion
of it all isn't what
I'm good at—world,
you goad a mouth
from this solitary
body and we forge
the language I need
to feel good where
storms sweep
the couch
and the notes
swell unsung.

To the attic

Many people try
to make history
pornography. There
are others who cry
in the corner of a room
designated for a purpose
other than crying. When people
cry it is customary to comfort
them. When people
are comfortable
they can resume
destruction. I remember
a couch burning snow
into retreat, a body
reclined on a picnic table,
night crawling up
to the attic. The cold past
is a message whose purpose
I can't decipher. Instead
I cut this eggplant
wide open.

Callus or grave

Windows traversed
by towels anonymous
as roads rope
some fear in with
a menu of lines
preordained and
algorithmic along
the muscles I use
to get there. In this way
I am like everyone,
I preserve the interests
that tie my shoes
to my feet and make
me go someplace
exchanging this or that
for a plastic cup
with ice that melts
when the other liquid's
gone. The laundromat
centralizes information
offsite and there
are symbols a sentence
could adopt to point
it out but I would
need a language
and the sky is not yet
thrown open, brick frames
bound to each other
with a callus
or a grave. In the meantime
I can take leisure
for a ride, buy a smoothie
on the corner and drink
it on a bench, I can think

about what power
I endow as I enjoy
taste, remember
pine trees, rain
and the death and rot
of other organisms
around the roots.

The museum

I have complicated feelings
about the museum. At night
outside its walls cast bright
by its special relationship
with light I understand
it holds a lot of art that
I don't really understand
yet. There are jets that we
can thank god are broken
and dysfunctional and there
are bankers that we can hope
spend the rest of their lives
in their own basements
eating chips. I think these
moments of pretend fog
cut through the poem to make
it a better representation
of nature tipping the scales
this side of capital. I help
myself to thinking what's
wrong with the museum
without taking action because
I am mesmerized by its obsidian
silence or its muted innards
making no moves to complicate
my understanding of their
significance and how they may
become important for the
preservation or slow bleeding
of civilization's pretend amble
into gated parking lots where
once I looked under the seats
for some change. I could be wrong
and the museum would still

swallow sound and light whole
as the traffic outside of it recedes
and perishes for another round
the engines vocalize to say I'm
going places and you're not art
and you don't get it, which is true
because I don't. There's a park
behind the museum and from
the top of that park where the
grass is rotten and embarrassing
the bare hill you can see
the dome the museum shoves
into the trajectory birds desire
and at night, when my feelings
about museums tangle up my
thoughts on civilizational
modes of trying to make it alright,
the bare hill is the preferred stance
from which to see art becoming air
and the birds get dumber
as our texts invade their
heartbeats and I forget
about the money I don't have
to visit the special exhibition
underneath the branches.

Flood line

Sometimes I think
that I'm going to be
dead one day
as trees merge
with floodwaters
and all the trouble
it is to think. Some people
will need to remember
each other whether
they like it or not
while oysters
continue to unite
on stones a shadow
obscures, smokestacks
a mask for open sky
taking it all in like
my mind would
if I didn't need to keep
names and times
in it for other people,
places aren't
themselves, don't
act like it when
we return. Debris
in floodwater
churns my inner life
settling on a face
and the words it uses
to make sure no mistake
has been made.
The weight
of a mountain,
and a neighbor's moan
intrude like flood lines

that mark important
points I haven't grasped
yet. These people
and their interests
and concerns
order snacks
before taking a nap,
the coins of the ear
gather for a potential
phone. I eat
a little animal
that came
from nameless ocean,
and a rag
comes along after,
a tide swiped across
the table.

We live

The bad dream
was an airport
the dead father
walked the terminal
and dolphins
at the periphery
feeling bureaucracy
as the bone's
motion, cough
the fog carries
only as sound
as what I could
remember
the dream
it's very dark there
the dolphins
or the dead father
the page becomes
an experience of, we
can point
to pieces disassembled
an empire of calculators
where we live
and this is my friend
the edge of the sun.

Reflection index

Out here
it's cold
crows
for miles
the inhale
exhale of trains
a mountain
I could forget
going bare
without even a leaf
or snow. Sometimes
growing old
the poems
dry out
referring in name
to a year that wasn't
the poems
we insist
it was. It's amusing
anyways
and what else
do we make
to keep warm
but the reflection
of the thing
called sun
indexing what
comes out
page-ready
so you can fence in
these concerns,
metaphor
forthcoming
hallucinations get

lucrative or the
road disguises
fissures with tar.

What I think is next

I used to sit alone
on long train rides
up the coast—a narrative
poem and rocks—I sat with
a person once and fell
asleep and when I woke
the person's head was
on my shoulder, it was
the first touch I had felt
in a long while because
I used to sit alone and
structure my day in
the tide watching how far
or close the water came
and how naked the
mud. Whenever Hendrix's
"Crosstown Traffic"
came on my father
would tell the story
of a friend of his who
fell asleep drunk
and face down in mud
until a car drove over
him but the mud was
soft enough that he
was fine, tire tracks
across the back of his
leather jacket like in the
song. A hand on the stairwell,
vandalism in the morning sun dividing
glare that jets up into the poem
catching impressions in the mouth
where words come and go. At dawn
when I am unsure if there

will be a world of tree and
parking lot behind the curtain
my body decides to be awake
and it makes sense to stop
moaning into the mold of what
I think is next. He also used
to tell this story about throwing
flaming objects at cops in Boston.

Under the Wallpaper

The song is about
stepping off a train
and walking across
the tracks onto a road
and seeing there is no
sidewalk and knowing
the road dissolves
at the edges, wet toilet
paper and sand stolen
from a crab's mouth. It's not
about feeling sorry that you
don't know where to put
your feet or who to ask
for a ride into the town
the other side of the hill
that may be only a hotel
with a bar where they ask
you your favorite beer and
carry hot french fries on a tray
to empty tables where someone
will soon sit. It's not that there
was a place where the hands
could get underneath the
wallpaper and make it clear
that there is more work to do
today before you can see anyone
you know until there is a knock
at the door, driftwood slamming
the side of a boat whose engine
has died in the harbor. Whatever
room could save you from the road
that climbs and then goes limp
at the intersection where police
sleep in their cars is now a room

that boxes fill, their walls sagging
and ugly to imitate the room
the house can barely hold. Whatever
room there was, the song is not
about that, instead it's about the cars
that don't stop and the phone call
that goes silent in your hand, the train
repeating stations towards the skyline
you were dumb enough to abandon.

Labors misshapen

But the scenery that came
and went was spray bottle
starlight bending without
regard for what a poem does
to swim beneath it charged with
the end spelled in rust. I don't want
to be music either partitioned
between afterthoughts carved from
bay light that isn't aesthetics because
it imprints blindness on my
sightlines until inside the library
it all becomes the chairs
and desks that I will then
look at for a little while. I also
don't want to be the poet
that makes it helping
to shape the hamburgers
of the future while there's time
not to die for labors misshapen
and altogether haunting
the laundry dirty. Poems
befriend roaches hiding until I sleep
because I also don't want
to start another sentence
that elaborates on rust
and death and the lot we saw
where the car died long ago
across from the power plant
that hums stillness as it negates
all stillness pretending it's ok.

Other currents

Of the opiated
masses I can only
say that I'm one
of them and it's fun
sometimes, music
does laps around
the edge of a wine
glass and I forget
how to be one person
this room to the next
one. Certain days
split open and leave
husks on each other's
floors, warm meals
for a mouth, there
are always police
where nobody
wants them
like a thought
scurrying to unwise
conclusions across
the table's distance
the ocean-wide
response registers
that we impress
each other. It's fun
to break laws and it's nice
to hear coffee dissolve
inside the grinder,
whose definition
departs in other
currents while I look
out the window
at the lake watching

stoplights fail. The end
comes believing
in itself, a receipt
and an apple
half eaten on the train
the jingle someone's
pocket emits
crowding the mouth
of an escalator.

Escape from the dining room

Fragments
hold my body
in place making
excess the shadow
I always thought
it was until verse
goes unconscious
walks into walls
escaping the dining rooms
and gardens I was promised
with the others
who would meet me there.
In the station
where we find our narrator
bright air slices
sightlines, a commuter
does stuff with his day
and makes sure
to pencil the tide
around the bunkbeds
of a prison without
an address, an insect
hallway evening
and fans that snore.
In Virginia I saw
the jobless legions
of snakes enjoying life,
boats or commerce
and the river tides
biting the dirt
and the shoreline
that bit back.

The Mountain

The mountain
and the one
who remembers
the mountain,
the valleys like
mouths catching
rain, the water
that was incorrect
an old boat that
could not correct
the water as stung
the skin swelled
a place along the
banks of a river
a cable or they are
roots I step over
a gunshot and
some birds, the fence
a sin we could
deposit on a beach
whose sands were
thrown through
a thousand front doors
locked with words
like house and habitat
a hand dismantling
a doorknob draws
new borders and
what's that a table
and the light in the hall?

Mist

The mist
between buttonholes
where skin
flashes and presses
the heart
and the brain
we use to move
the legs and make
them go a place,
the legacy of a throne
in our heads says
stop that do something
else. The glass repaired
to be this window
people speak behind,
the fits of a hand,
a notepad.
The phone emits light
someone spits
before going dark
and you wait
on a bench in gray
after work as mist
unshackles treetops,
a sky we forgot was there.

Motorcycle heartbeat

Sun is the cheese
shuttling off to be
alone with empty
chairs in a room
dim as a bear. Sleep
heralds a brain I can
use again to put makeup
on the dead leaves swollen
and wet where the moss
reclaims a sweater
and I feel like a floatation
device with nobody on it
helping myself to a tide
that returns like a slow
heartbeat or a motorcycle
in traffic on the bridge.

Market of hills

Poem city
broke the crane
and swung it low
to lit earth glass-veined
and discounted as sweet
starvation could be
the hour's collapse.
Sunday asphalt and we
nod to the hair
of the dog that carries
a noise around no one
can hear. Take this
body to a house
built on names
and lay me down
a title I will abandon
hills for no one's
market where the barges
mark the outer seams
ambition couldn't break.

Doors

Whose basketball
does this vending
machine hide
and how do I make it
back to the holes
the motions open,
abundance
and its syntax
calling time out.
Words pantomime
transactions
so I learn new
slang, disintegration
settles the accounts,
walls or horizons
the antennae graph.
This time
won't be like
last week's poison
read aloud on the air
unfolding as a scroll
whose breath
is an amazing
hard drive
the lint will clog. We can
shock-treat that promised
future back
to reality, stopwatch
arbiters of crane-work
grind their teeth
as helicopters
lower.

Running Late

If I wish death
on the departing
bus, the empty
rooms I arrive late
to will forgive me,
my feet a pain
in the ass that was
a good seat
at the donut counter
a penny in the tray
along the wind's
shredded body. Hurt
in the mouth of the fog
my thinking wants
an emergency exit
a pathway whose air
grows cold the closer
to the water's market
we become, falling
for negative space. What if
forgiveness is a ruse
and the floor
is not that rumbling
bed the surface
of the river made it out
to be. I'm tired
and I need to learn
new tricks not to disperse
myself along paths
between letters
illegible in their glow.

Soft yonder

Seagulls make
their rounds
as the mind's aporia
squares this flock
with a line
that meets another
line to weave
a place into being still
a picture of buildings
and mailboxes
by the road's
edge. I say
don't get lost
there in the gaps
between the body
and the currents a soft
yonder of trees exerts,
a church steeple
never slouching
where rain
drives. When the sun
darkens there's a feeling
of seeing myself
in a picture I didn't
know was taken years
ago, an anchor lifted
from memory's erasure
the day dislodged
from its moorings,
boards instead of windows
across the road from
where I grew up,
cops driving past.

No coupon

It's ok not to want
to see yourself
reflected on the surface
of a city that
used to be a city, the sea
nipping its ankles
negating the whole
idea. An amusement park
screams like the airplane
that brought us
here, branched
lattice work throwing
a leaf in your face
and then charging you
for it. A cat, the mouth
of an empty bottle
alive with a history
of hands shaping an ache
around the bends
of an alphabet.

Fugitive debris

Machines gather
the fractured periphery
into a bridge that
shudders being crossed
by fugitives we call
feelings, sky's timepiece
eliciting another word
from the people we elect
to step on us. I haven't yet
gotten to the point
where I know
how to make thought
not worry about
vacated property
hosting moths that
have nothing to eat
flutter in face
when I just want to get
a little work done
without the blockades
such feelings erect
between obligations
to those in front of me
and those I only
read about. Buried in
whatever debris comprises
what already happened
there is a neighborhood
by a river and some trains
and injustice howl
a tune together, I used to
park there and smoke
with friends and listen
as porchlight punctured
a map someone's head
bent to see.

I found a fossil

There are barriers
that people heave closer
to our bodies
making the edges
shiver, and these
lines people
call them borders
proliferating there
where you can't
see them, that person
you're speaking to is
a wall fossilized
around bullets
and loose change. In the
daylight air smells
like cigarettes that had
a mouth, I walk along
the shoreline
and interrupt some
cormorants who are busy
with a mating ritual
and won't understand
these problems, grease
stains on paper plates the sun
colors where it touches
bird feet. People want
to talk but I can't
do that either, men
with guns make the rounds
on the balconies of the college
and tell each other jokes
that no one thinks
are funny and I start
to think these must be

the avenues that will
host the lines
of reasoning
that follow me around
that ask me to analyze
and fear things
at the same time. Defying
these mandates we can
carve across and within
the fences a place
with a TV, many channels
and a rug.

Nature Poem

There's a field over there
where someone's cut down all the trees
but there's this one tree at the crest of a hill
looking down at the rest of the trees that someone
cut down and the sun is shining
and the last remaining tree
is soliciting a poem. It's important
to listen to trees and to write
nature poems when moved to write
nature poems by the rest of the trees
that now are dead in the dirt
and are not coming back to life ever, but rather
hosting the types of life forms
that like it when other things die
so that they can be alive, such as
mushrooms. Once when
I was younger I ate mushrooms and took
my clothes off in a forest and I remember
how warm the sun felt on my skin
but how strange my friends were
feeling until they took their clothes off too.
Later in the day we stared at a creek
long enough to have our perception
encompassed entirely by the algae
which glowed red through
the hours that stole away the afternoon
and hid it from us in a car at the edge of the forest
with the sun and us coming down. That is an experience
that I think might be worthy
of a nature poem. As for the dead trees, there is
a phantom called commerce
that some men somewhere think they
need to keep alive and so
they make phone calls from large towers

or from offices inside their homes, they laugh
at each other's jokes in a bar or restaurant
where earlier in the day when the sun hadn't yet
sold all the hours short for some
other coordinates they made reservations
because otherwise the wait for a table
or a spot at the marble counter
is much too long and who has
time for that. I am equally capable of keeping
commerce alive like feeding fumes to some flame
that eternally burns because we believe in its virtues
and its power to clear the land for more
space where we can erect walls inside of which
we will continue to discuss commerce
and the sufficiency of our food
when we weigh the taste against its
price. There is a tree
on the hill's pinnacle
glowing red through the hours the sun
gives it from the west
where other things are dying in addition
to trees. As much as I think
commerce is violence and a phantom
worth vanquishing I don't know
if I will ever be capable of crafting
an effective nature poem but in that field
there's still one tree left and it's testing the air.

II.

It's ok

It's ok
to hate the fourth
of July
don't look at me
thinking I feel good
about the heat stained
with grease smoke
an empty street corner
or a stray
car whose driver forgot
not to go to work,
but I do admit
to happiness when
the street is empty
and nothing
is convenient, the trash
uncollected
inspires hope
we can stay lazy
tomorrow too
and limp to refrigerators
I wouldn't eat that
if I were you, families
and friends rearranging
fragments of law. For now
the worst part is the work
it all takes
not to think about
bombs with a hot dog
in your mouth.

Official ash

No salad bar
can save us,
sweaty and faceless
the dark
speaks a route
and the body
a measure
of the road's
mutation beyond
what's visible
and loud. I can't
hold the mind
in place long enough
to feel, a defense erects
feeble distraction
like look at this
issue of a magazine
out of print
two decades ago,
this music whose
rasp measures
the wear and pain
dirt can churn
if you look
at the land
and just think
about the past
a little. Lodged
there are water
buckets measuring
shadows against
hunger, I have a mess
to put in order
tomorrow, a drain

that won't leak,
an envelope to stamp,
a grocery whose
price rises, a state
with camps
and prisons, we run
from fire's
claim on the dark, surpluses
left behind as official
ash. A bank opens
in the morning
receives my check,
a hand holds a wire
to bend the will
and the mosquitoes
get what blood
is theirs before we kill them
waiting for justice
in a parking lot.

Thinking Fragments

Thinking fragments
to remember
that language is
supposed to remember
a vague gift
that corrodes. Sometimes
memory hurts my back
and I excuse
myself to recover
what fears
can be depended on
to move dawn's goalpost
deeper into fog. But the man
in the suit really
was following me
from one side of the rally
to the other
as I shuffled my body
between others
lobbing chants
at the windows
of empty offices.

No thanks

It isn't good
when you know
somebody is eating
dinner on top
of your head but
it may be wise to live
with it for a while
or at least as long
as you can, sweating
across the parking lot
where bay waters lurk
and the day shelters
pine needles stabbing
themselves a shadow
where the light blinds
you to omens hidden
in the last thing anyone
said to you, hello
or you have a stain
on your shirt. One doesn't
develop feelings of adoration
or appreciation for those
inclined towards jailing
others and you try not
to think that there may
be a crumb on the floor
where there was a carpet,
you could lay down there
when the sun hits
its patterns as if you had
a patch of grass and you can
speak to the no one who's there
so none of the words
that you use can become

anyone else's and you can distract yourself from the crumbs that become your responsibility to either eat or clean up.

COPIES

Over the objections
of the other brain
I have I make a copy
of the document
and save one for myself,
the building could burn
down tomorrow before
I return—we should
be so lucky—have
a little more sun tan
lotion. I have a name
that identifies me
to others and keeps
track of my movements
in a conversation
I can't hear,
that anchors me
in documents
stamped and moved
into a drawer I can't
see. It isn't important. Air
opens its gates to wind's
horse rearranging sounds
we probably don't want
heads turn upwards
to be momentary
salutations like long lost
icebergs colliding into one.

Democracy robe

I like it when my
cell phone sends a signal
to people who want to watch
me so that the people who
want to watch me can then
watch me. It's like bending
a mirror to shoot the sun
back into the sky
where people who
want to watch me
think they live. I noticed
the poem like a muscle
tightening in a tunnel
under the river. I like
to stand around for hours
inside a cage and chant
about democracy. The next
station is a cavity in the earth
that doesn't need a filling. I can't
say what I plan to do with the
language I've learned from
the one and only source of light
on the surfaces that conceal
discontent in the hollow cavities
of the world. If the world were
a body its medical robe would
fall into oblivion
with all our loose change
jangling in the pockets.

Against the Music

It's like if we become
like paper we'll fit in between
the flames and make it
alright to the office. Sometimes
I have to remember who I am
and write straight to the thing
there is to say about sleet
rubbing up against the music
that enters the skull cold
enough to take a break
from speaking and say
hallelujah there is less
money shadowing all our
help desk interactions than
there was yesterday. The porch
light stays fog smudged
and a luxury liner flashes
the bay starch white to make
my feelings lift off the floor
of the earth where squirrels
motion for the exits they've
made from a season shredded
wide open like a trick. If you
enter the realm of feeling
a hand on a rusty doorknob
then you'll get lost among shapes
the dumb birds carve trying
to get out of your way
remembering who they
could have been.

If you want a boss

If you want
a boss you should
go shopping, they were all
chewing gum and discussing
the boats that traverse the page
en route to discipline
and stomach cramps. I said
hello to someone whose boss
I became in the aisles where
bulb flickers hint at the next
world and the jaw tightens without
discipline or fatigue. Presidents
make bad neighbors
and worse friends, the clothes
slacken in the room
bosses sponsor, you speak
a little to ordain a threat
that will be used against
you in evaluations
or bar rooms where
nobody smokes. There were
geese losing number
carrying this latitude to
a soft earth that can
soothe any stomach cramp
and then there were
fewer geese doing
that and then there were
none. Nobody really knows
what it means.

Biting our lips

They moved
to a different city
and meanwhile
I am swallowed
incorrectly by this
one. There used to be
emails biting
our lips to remember
who it was. We'll
get used to the traffic
aching outside the names
we used to have.

Poem

Yeah but I am
no one's dirt bag
even though
one day I could be
if I try hard enough.
The land
and the sky
a wide singing mouth
printed on the money
I spend. A song
that rumbles like a train
cold water
the drooling windows
drop on my head.

Losing the thread

Don't include
car horn, subway
train, don't swallow
a language
glossed in motions
you control
and do not control
it's Sunday go for a walk,
Wednesday try
to wake up,
dishes fall, a room's
precipice
no metaphor can
stand. Speak your
salaried mind
as a room with bills
a poem invades
ravage what motion
they make, a hole
where a fence
meets dirt no one
can imitate,
a coffee mug
with a slow leak
and the stain
that was a thought
as you walk a turnstile
or gate losing
the thread
speaking patterns repeat
yeah pretty good
and you as the caesura
opens finding
no dock, no fog
and not even
a moving tide.

Capture regular

Heat presses
a domesticated
blur and summer
poems rattle thoughts
left behind fleeing
capture. There are
feelings I'm not allowed
to voice, the air
and anger imagined
words hold, just wait
here while I hide
in the post office. As
any flag knows,
hatred takes
the tone forgetting
knew and the shipwreck
waits as people shove
straws into iced coffee,
the land their feet trod
an archive rattling old jaws
to speak the nostalgia
of glaciers lit screens
flash making
capture regular. I have to
wait a minute
while my files load
some work I'm encouraged
to complete, opinions
in the gardens
with artwork
and sleep. The envelope's
taste is a station wagon's
backseat, I take
memory's component

parts walking, the sun hot
and anger sweeter than
blank space the mind
traverses, headlights
or headlines missing
the point entirely.

Useless and good

It's possible
to have a job
that allows you
to forget the existence
of a past, days
the cars carried
wobbly towards
tenuous conclusions
a misplaced line
that ends at an
uncomfortable desk.
What's possible
isn't really what's
desirable and you can
take the notebook
with you to work
and use it for purposes
that do not
advance the mission
of the organization
for which you work,
move pages backwards,
reaching the front
cover before
the bus stop and the hair
that stands in wind. Rules a text
follows hide ruins
in the floor, there
are other lives
where we walk,
philosophers living
and dying talk
to degraded stones
that others build

fences around, five
dollars at the door. If you
forget your job
there will be space
to breathe the dust
that runs the public
square, veiling a mountain
and the conversations
at the peak useless
and good.

Narrative Shell

Tractors engage
in the production
of the beach
but my body
erodes it, the moon
I mention by name
absorbs the white
light of its lettering
so I engage the body
in the production
of poems degrading
a sky how water
does breaking
around my body
shedding obligations
to land and its concern
absorbed in production.
On the way I pilfer feelings
about the body
and put them in what's
made and do what I can
to conceal its making. I can be
afraid of being good
at the smooth operation
the world hosts when
we're good but
thinking stopped being
helpful, long lost
to narrative shells.
How to think this all
away so a moment
can enter enjoyment
far from lines
a laptop emulates

and the person
whose body can't be detail
crosses the park
whose construction
concluded long ago
and made a beach,
activity obscured
by headlights that
churn sand
out from under my feet.

I WON'T BE AT THE MEETING

Yeah but I won't be at the meeting
so you should write to me
before tomorrow and reschedule
the meeting that I'm not going to
attend. The meeting
is tomorrow but I won't be there
so you should contact me using
any form of written communication
that suits you, I won't reschedule it for you
because it isn't my place
to go around telling people
how their time should be filled. It's fine for you
to talk to me now, though I for one
don't quite see the point because
I won't remember a word you're saying,
it's too late in the evening
for me to worry about the time tomorrow
the meeting will be and I don't have any children
so that won't be a concern but at any moment
one can become afflicted with any
number of ailments be they nerves or nausea
or food poisoning from the food consumed
between the last two meetings when I kicked
my colleague's shin hard enough to bruise it
underneath the table and didn't
say sorry. I don't have time to reschedule
the meeting tonight because sleep
is upon me so it's up to you
to reschedule the meeting which in any case
won't take place until tomorrow so you
have plenty of time to prepare your documents
and tell me what the organization will look like
in minute detail six or seven months from now
when the meeting that's scheduled for today

won't matter anymore. If you email me this evening
I will check my email in my morning misery
and make your own misery my top priority,
I feel indebted to you for scheduling
a meeting because I know how
time can be quick as a bleeding nose
in the winter night knowing the pillow disappears
before the meeting which has been canceled,
the noises in the distance distinct from the
heartbeat guiding my schedule closer
to its ultimate collapse which comes
when the seagulls that prop up the sky
get sick of monitoring our motions
and we scavenge the shore
where our jobs once were.

III.

Short circuit harmony

Exilic trajectory
put me in the car
and I am stuck
on the other side now
a caesura, then
stones of guilt
sweat inner space
not having phoned,
dislocation lifts fog
without number
I can't see. Why say
more, the oppositions
of the world cohere
to reclaim the uttered
complaint I've felt since
the beginning
compelled to
short circuit
whatever harmony
settles good enough
for suckers. The night
the gas ran out the farms
dispersed as cities
that kept their mouths
shut and I felt
rain slap a window
and Dylan's voice
made me tired of it
and taught me to lie,
but what else
can a story say beyond
the windowsill, the curtain
and I'm sorry
or something like it.

Reliable shadows

Smug radio voice
pleads a dumb case
but I like the
Abdel Halim Hafez
CD better, so for
violins and ouds
the houseflies
get to work trying
not to die. Far off
poets write to me,
say be careful
not to get bitten,
personality goes
on strike, voids
cascade applause,
the song begins
and the soup
runs low as if
my hunger right now
were a joke. Tomorrow's
train ride practice
will yield little
in the way of singular emotion,
broken strings
fingers try to discipline
can't sing a past
the song didn't know it had
and more work
falls from the sky
as reliable shadows
chart the wattage
I am provided on loan,
a screen door
and dry dirt, the yard
the fire escape became.

Bone highway

I ended up
doing the things
I didn't want
to do, I did them
and after that
other things
that I also
didn't want to do
but I did those
things too.
A calendar
is the bad kind
of technology
leaves, a windshield
a big highway
that never
resolves itself
and remains troubled
with bones. When I do
what I don't want
to do I don't
have to worry
about bones
or highways,
calendars
or their violence.

Treadmill daylight

Have some dangerous
coffee, tell me, what's
death like, unearth
muffled voices
the other side
of the wall the trees
outside fling
a storm overturns
the horizon's
windowed rule
swallowing available
words that could be
used for a garden poem
tactless as war time
or the holidays
of sour milk. But the porch
is nice this afternoon
hosting a parade
of sweat to confuse the brain
about which hours
slip away from our feet
like treadmill daylight
fucking with the balance
an hour could cop. Fresh
grass caught
in a beard, flies
transmit sounds
as satellite mannerisms
we forsake for birds
at dumb day's end.

Social dirt

How long
do I have to
wait, where
did I put human
connection,
under sweat
that slides down
an unearthed
word I hesitate
to speak to people
negotiating trash
on the parkway. Days
or weeks stream
lexical miles
that moments at a desk
grip and compress
for easier digestion
than thinking
something through.
The steam train got stuck
as the hill collapsed
around it in the 1920s
the bones are
still in there,
and the riverbank
is the same. It isn't
that hard to imagine
not going back
to anything that
already happened,
the shared rooms
where gesticulating
limbs fertilize social dirt
for exchange. The outer

rim of conversation
exceeds capture
but what satellite
carries the remainder,
work until your
throat hurts, the yawns
and the dark bookend
lyrics the moment
they're written.

To be alive

Goddamnit
life on earth
why are you
dying all the time
and then it isn't
that bad
fireplaces
dishware the wealthy
put on the curb
for me to take
home, think
about the sickness
dust carries
and wash it off
back to the earth
I want to
yell didn't you
know we've
been taught
to be alive
unconditionally
and to enjoy
any air that passes
the windowsill
domestic creep
pulling a line
expect indigestion
and cramps
living a time
people talk about
in rooms
that haven't been built yet.

Only voids

If there were
an eraser
for consciousness
I would have only voids
that converge
to form a desk
where my hands
can rest. Let's go back
to what wasn't this
imaginary fiber
bending to winds that press
more terror into
radio knobs tossing
imitation politics
into a body to grace
the static. What I was
supposed to do
but didn't was pay
a bill and simulate
abundance, make
a sandwich
for lunch. It's good
that there are
eyes that water coughing
on the dust public transit
renders as commerce
in the blindness
the scenery encourages
as sirens gulp
without rage
or purpose. If the first
thing I say sounds
terrible and if I write
the terrible thing

on the rattling
table I make air abandon
its imitation and expose
frames that shape
my ability to see
the ice on the lake
without telling anyone
what it's good for
or what they can do with it
to further develop their skills.

Stone morning

A doorknob
on the sidewalk
an imprint
the conversation
interrupts saying
I'm caffeine contorting
thought
into empty barrels
on algae's stones
marked with names
each one a register
of the inability
to imagine help
arriving in due time,
morning time on stones
this is my bed
and it doesn't work
very well, snow
filtering sightlines
impossible as knowing
what I don't want
to do anymore.

Dispersal order

It's hard
to decide
which I like
better, the sea
or the brain
as both are domains
that most people
don't know very much
about and are
therefore more
interesting than other
topics like luggage
or hit songs playacting
revolution tomorrow
which opens instead
as a garbage truck's
mouth small enough
for the alleyway. You can
use what you
don't know about your brain
like an iron tool
whose use and origin
escape you.
The brain submerges
itself in the sea,
songs inaudible
beneath waves
and the detritus
a thought produces
disperses like a story
you fall asleep telling.

Number one bus

My favorite bus driver
drives the number one
bus and when he pulls
close to the curb he is
smoking a cigarette which
is prohibited
behavior according
to metropolitan transit
authority rules
and regulations.
When passengers board
the bus he sometimes tells
them to hurry up and
without warning closes
the door on stragglers
who have one foot
on the first step
and the other on the
street. I don't know why
this is my favorite bus driver
but often I think
about this city's
police state bloodlust
for anyone whose hunger
is a sentence we can't speak
without running out of breath.
There are desks where some
get paid to be watched
and keep track of certain
information while others get paid
to do the watching, and behind
other windows radiators
on soggy floors open
to cold front whimsy through

the boards. I guess for reasons
like this the man who drives
the number one bus
and violates most rules
appeals to me. The number one bus
passes the frozen beach
where one day last summer
after the park rangers decided
the ocean was closed
everyone went
back in all at once like waves
going in the opposite direction.

The boats

The boats passing
in the bay
are an idea somebody
had once
the building where
people fetch water
at prearranged hours
to avoid
speaking to each other
has space
one can rent
for a reasonable
monthly rate, we can
think about it
and make decisions
later when the heat
isn't dulling all
our senses. Railroad
trajectories and gravel's
subtle rattle, the water's
residue on the hull
of the boat, contracts
both parties
forgot to sign. There are
rooms along the way
vessels where you
can hear someone
speak, the walls thin
enough for anyone
to spy on anyone else,
and after a little
while some sleep,
smoke dissipating above.
Tomorrow they will

go somewhere else
by land and water
with a little less money
than they carried today.

Tomorrow baby

If we say
it's just getting
worse, let's not have
children, then it isn't
clear which nation
or rusted barrel
we're talking about
they're dangerous
and they will both
make you sick. A poem
leaves a legacy
on the bridge, drugs
were involved in its
composition and still
it's very difficult
for a poem to contort
itself to a nation's
chain link board games
where escape
into the checkout aisles
is golden as hope
behind the wheel
swallowing our despair,
heavy traffic. I think
I still like to watch
the boats enter the port
with a heavy load
for the power
plants, I think the gulls
are smart to cloud
the wake the boat
churns where fish
go belly up like desires
overstaying their

welcome. The tomorrow
babies cry, the shore
rusts to become
the ghost of a meal
no one can afford and still
the stadium glows.

Aquatic leash

Everything crawls
a difficult path on the
common skin
of a dark sea
while we await
shelter before night
comes and the water
goes into hiding.
The ambiguous to be
of being someone's
eternal debt becomes
a poem across wind
I invented not to get
paid and then
a phone rings
behind the bar. I overdid
the positioning
of wires among the sand
that veils them,
an escape the mind's
leash can't discipline
like children
after they're finished
walking incorrectly.
How can we be sure
the script says we're
ready, I drop coins
on a tray as boats
depart the surface
of the aquarium
that passes for a harbor.

Part of the Story

I am not
the fury
I thought I could
be, tossing
newspaper to flames
the wagging trees
canopy, only part
of the story
when the limes
grow complacent,
and sunlight's
own branch
splits the brain
free to find a new
purpose tying
shoelaces. To verify
my identity I breathe
a little louder
air become muscle,
satellite noise
before the signal
changes, ambulatory
sunset where the trees
can't be.

Unknown or Better

The blisters on skin
become skin and then
you don't notice
that it's alright not to
notice, thought
earns the right
to enclose possible
channels, this
is the way language
gathers matter
into its fold,
an old bridge
the cars can't use
and then forget it
you get a discount
for nostalgia. The ruins
of a place that used to
hold cannons
and shot at invading
idiots are much
better unknown
as ruins these words
can hide pretending
they know something
else. I am no one's
specimen studied
in no lecture hall,
the face of a speaker
lined as lava, the way
the drunk's face sunk
into itself atop
the barstool to open
space for some other sleep
fumbling harmony.

Lyric's yawn

One reason
not to want to die is
for those who are living
the dead are such
a pain in the ass, we have
to spend all our time
remembering them
missing the bus all aglitter
with medicinal
sunlight. It doesn't hurt
to sit around
a table with others
and think things
through, violins
stroked in the corner
a text message
sinking in the abyss
where wine
fragments, falls. The airport's
a terrible place. I couldn't
speak to the woman
behind the ticket
counter as a phantom
mess clogged
all my inner channels
sad they couldn't
say a thing. I'd like
to think a better
dissonance than today's
density green
and bleeding birdcalls
and stairwells top
to bottom, the train car's
alliance of headphones

where I run late
with grease stains
on my pants. I think
it's better to go back
home and give up
tell the driver
to stop the train
rip through the zipper
a hedge whose
language is hourly,
we get a family
whose town goes
missing, but these
are books, stick around
and pull on a back
and fall onto
an empty street, we can
read them and never
become tired lyrics
of an anthem everyone
agrees to ridicule.

Screening room

Books and rugs
from other
countries are
in the car's trunk
and as twigs
and animal
hair from our
heads fill a room
I leave. Sometimes
this music video comes
back to me, the singer
leaves a payphone
hanging in a hallway
institutional white
lyric mouth and a
dial tone that wasn't.
Once upon a time
anarchists and
communists lived
in the apartments
this town built
with no one's help
but hardly anyone
remembers or knows
why it isn't part
of the architecture
our thinking
takes in, train south
and the river's
flood levels swallow
some land undigested.
The school house
in the town I left
was red and inside

I tutored a child
whose apartment
didn't have winter
heat, I helped
him read and to know
what he was
reading, a bulldozer
down the street
answered silence
between question
and answer like who
wants to know?

On the roof

On the roof
I felt a tower
go up in my ear
a conversation
I had to rearrange
into digestible
segments pleading
with my conscience
to find the right place
and interject. A steel rod
runs this place visible,
small animals scare
their own reflections,
a watery receipt
for how to plan this world
and who we can
hire to ache more
than us. Motion sick
daylight named itself
bright and singular,
social obligation
and the oral tide, a cave
I felt comfortable idling
within. Nobody was
terribly offended.

Other Machine
for Anders

I sit in the collective
café and play
backgammon
until Mars
is not a lamp, come
follow this flame
with me, summer
ducks where
the pond used to
wander. What haunts
is that which lifts
unwilling blur
out of an old bed
and I can't forget
the keys or the picture
of myself I carry
in case anyone forgets
my name. T-shirts
are on sale today
and cars ditch the street
for bread and some
other machines.

On art

I still don't know
if I like art
as much as
I like the word
art. Magic subtle
slides between
teeth of the will. It's
that art has
number, a loud colony
insists its walls
keep quiet, busy now
and busy tomorrow.
Winter there isn't a
place to produce
the outside the inside
defines and it would be
easier if instead
of a word art were
some kind of fruit
ripened where
it grows so I could
eat it and then
be done with this
conversation.

Stone noise

Sometimes when I listen
to punk rock it isn't
the songs themselves
that feel familiar, instead it's that
somebody else out there has been
as angry as I don't think
I can ever let myself
be again. Look at the police
or think about the state
or think about how much
money a person can make
by making others fatally ill
and how many other people's
pensions are rooted
so deeply in this diffuse complex
of cause and effect
and then maybe it will become
clear to you why there is
in the first place some anger
that can't find expression
except in songs that find legitimacy
by being songs and therefore
a safer expression of whatever threat
might have otherwise
materialized. If a person knows
how to grow and cook rice in many
fields the globe hosts
and if another set of people know
how to teach that person
how to hypnotize themselves
then the set of people with
the hypnotism skills
will outwit the ones
who grow and cook rice

without anyone knowing
the difference. Nice billboard city
with noise even between
stones, I became
less plagued there by the anger
for which I found expression,
meaning that if you listen long
and let the air tighten cold around you
then you may realize
what temptation there is
in memory for me because
that stone noise is where
some fell deeply enough
that their letters home
couldn't reach the surface
for their troubles clouding
the paths. I've also always thought
punk rock can legitimize
anti-social tendencies
that can't be good
and may even alienate
some of my closest friends
as it dawns on them that in the furthest
reaches of my thoughts
it's easy to criticize most
everything existing
and to get tangled in criticism
so that I think being bound by it
is the only fertile ground
from which to think. But that
can't be right.

Legible heights

Recomposition
starts from thrown
light the train
enters leaving
the tunnel as people
wait for ownership
after which time
there will be rest
and time to let
thought dissolve
headlines that
aren't real. The legibility
of talking
is what counts
and not the good guy
bad guy battle
exploding and invisible
between words I speak
to become
innovative idea
or a lunch break's
essential difference.
Get a life
and the train doors
close, satellites
net music from air
leftover after cold wind
maps names
onto storefronts
legible like sediment
chasing composition
and twitching
into place. No curtains
as the neighbors fold

shirts on the bedspread,
a signal fails
and I notice
the cheekbones
of others, aberration is no
longer a fire or its ash
but waking up
to notice a construction
site's shadow cuts
ambient sunshine poses,
we make narrative
out of this stuff but still
no clear line
from precipice
to shoe placed safely
on the curb. I make
coffee, figure a wrench
in the picture feelings
drew, other heights
the windows
marked brought
low to be
branch work. Sing the
doorstep resting place
that doesn't ask
for the dismissal
of other facades
netted and caught
by spreadsheet violence
making places
we walk and think
other to our bodies,
you can't have that
which you want
and you can't want that
without invisible

headlines submerged
as money beneath
a pillow. You breed
an ache or a twitch
and the head tries
to read, encase
a word in some thought
and handle fragments
the air abandoned
for signals en route
to common fire
across a map we
can't yet see.

Acknowledgments

My deepest gratitude to all of those who read and responded to this manuscript with generous comments, suggestions and praise: Daniel Owen, Barbara Henning, Lewis Warsh, Matvei Yankelevich, Anna Gurton-Wachter, Lisa Rogal. Thank you also to Pareesa Pourian for the beautiful illustration, to Bruno Gulli for listening to me read many of these poems after dinner, to Eddie Berrigan for the many conversations on process, and to Rebecca Manski for all manner of emotional support and intellectual exchange. Endless gratitude as well to Tod and Aurelia at Spuyten Duyvil for agreeing to publish this collection, and for their endless labor publishing so many great books over the years.

As with any written work, many of the poems in this collection were inspired or informed by a wide array of texts whose poetic, theoretical or aesthetic marks are likely evident throughout. Some of these works are: *Being Singular Plural* by Jean Luc-Nancy, Stevphen Shukaitis's *The Composition of Movements to Come,* Michael Hardt and Antonio Negri's *Assembly,* Kirill Medvedev's *It's No Good, Dis/Art, (This) Labor: Transfiguration in the Age of Precarity and Disposability* by Bruno Gulli, Alexander Vvedensky's *An Invitation for Me to Think,* George Oppen's *Of Being Numerous,* Amiri Baraka's *Transbluesency,* Jasper Bernes's *The Work of Art in the Age of Deindustrialization,* and many others. This is not to mention the many rich conversations that happen both in person and over email with a great many like-minded poets, writers and thinkers.

TONY IANTOSCA is a poet and educator living in Brooklyn, NY. His poems can be found in A Glimpse Of, Second Factory, 6x6, Lungfull!, a Perimeter, among other publications. He is the author of two chapbooks—*Naked Forest Spaces* (Third Floor Apartment Press, 2013) and *Team Burnout* (Overpass Books, 2013)—and a full length collection, *Shut Up, Leaves* (United Artists Books, 2015). He is a lecturer in the English department at Kingsborough Community College (CUNY) in Brooklyn, NY.

www.ingramcontent.com/pod-product-compliance
Lightning Source LLC
Chambersburg PA
CBHW030158100526

44592CB00009B/334